DIGITAL PARENTING

DR DHEERAJ MEHROTRA

Made with ♥ on the Notion Press Platform
www.notionpress.com

Contents

Preface v

1. Understanding Digital Landscape 1
2. Challenges To Digital Parenting 8
3. Parenting Secrets 17
4. Poem On Digital Parenting 71
5. Song On Digital Parenting 73
6. Quotes On Digital Parenting 76
7. Jokes On Digital Parenting 81
8. Tips To Fostering Healthy Tech-child Relationship 84

About The Author 95

Books By The Same Author 97

Preface

The digital age has revolutionized the way we communicate, learn, and interact with each other. It has brought about countless opportunities for personal and professional growth. Still, it has also introduced new challenges and risks that parents must navigate to ensure their children's safety and well-being.

Effective digital parenting has become more critical as school students increasingly rely on technology for communication, education, and entertainment. This book aims to give parents the knowledge, tools, and resources they need to raise responsible and resilient digital citizens.

Through research-based insights and practical advice, this book will address some of the most pressing issues facing parents of school students in the digital age, including cyberbullying, online privacy, digital addiction, and screen time management. It will also explore the benefits and potential drawbacks of various digital technologies, such as social media, video games, and educational apps, to help parents make informed decisions about their children's use of technology.

The book is organized into three main sections. The first section focuses on understanding the digital landscape and its impact on school students; the second section provides strategies for promoting responsible digital behaviour and minimizing risks. The third section offers guidance for navigating specific digital parenting challenges, such as dealing with online predators, managing social media use, and addressing cyberbullying.

Throughout the book, readers will find real-world examples, expert opinions, and practical tips to help them foster a healthy and balanced relationship between their children and technology. We hope this book will empower parents to confidently guide their children through the digital age, ensuring they have the skills, knowledge, and awareness to thrive in the digital world while staying safe and secure.

Author

www.authordheerajmehrotra.com

ONE

Understanding Digital Landscape

It is more necessary than ever for parents to take an active part in supervising their children's technology usage in today's increasingly digital environment. This is especially true for younger generations. Assisting children in developing safe and healthy behaviours while using technology is referred to as "digital parenting," and it is an essential component of contemporary parenting.

Understanding the digital landscape and its impact on school students is crucial for parents who want to foster a healthy and balanced relationship between their children and technology. The digital landscape constantly evolves, with new devices, platforms, and apps emerging rapidly. As such, parents need to stay informed about the latest trends and developments in the digital world to effectively guide their children through it.

The impact of technology on school students is multi-faceted. On the one hand, technology has the potential to enhance learning and provide students with new opportunities for personal and academic growth. Digital tools such as educational apps, online resources, and virtual learning environments can help students acquire new skills and knowledge and improve their academic performance.

On the other hand, excessive technology use can have negative effects on school students. Excessive screen time can lead to physical health issues such as obesity, poor posture, and eye strain. It can also have adverse effects on mental health, including increased rates of anxiety, depression, and sleep disturbances.

Moreover, technology can expose students to new risks and challenges, such as cyberbullying, online predators, and exposure to inappropriate content. As such, parents must be aware of the potential risks associated with technology use and take steps to mitigate them.

By understanding the digital landscape and its impact on school students, parents can make informed decisions about their children's use of technology. They can set appropriate boundaries and limits on technology use, encourage healthy behaviours, and teach their children about responsible digital citizenship. They can also take steps to protect their children from the potential risks of technology use, such as by monitoring their online activity and educating them about online safety and privacy. Understanding the digital landscape and its impact on school students is essential for parents who want to raise responsible and resilient digital citizens.

Children are introduced to various forms of technology at a very young age, demonstrating how deeply embedded technology has become in our everyday lives. According to recent research, toddlers as young as two already utilise mobile devices. Technology presents children with both opportunities and dangers. Options include access to educational resources, social connections, and entertainment. Dangers have the possibility of being exposed to inappropriate content. The practice of digital parenting may assist youngsters in securely and ethically navigating the internet environment.

Protecting children online should be one of your top priorities regarding parenting in the digital age. Children risk seeing inappropriate information, being bullied online, and being targeted by online predators when they go online. Parents with children who use digital devices must be aware of their children's dangers and take preventative measures. This might involve putting parental controls on devices, limiting the time kids spend in front of screens and teaching them how to be safe when using the internet.

When it comes to the use of technology, parents may also play a role in assisting their children in developing good habits. Excessive time spent in front of electronic media may adversely impact children's health and development, including increased risk of obesity, disturbed sleep patterns, and poor academic performance. Reading, playing outdoors, and spending time with family and friends are just some things that digital parents may encourage their children to participate in while still establishing limits for their children's screen usage.

Parenting in the digital age may help children learn critical life skills, improve safety, and encourage healthy behaviours. Children acquainted with technology will have a substantial edge in the employment market since technology plays an increasingly essential role in the workplace. Coding, digital design, and social media administration are all areas in which digital parents may assist their children in developing abilities. Parents also can inspire their children to utilize technology as a means of creative expression and to solve problems.

Setting an excellent example regarding technology utilisation is crucial to digital parenting. Children pick up behaviours by watching their parents, so if their parents are always on their phones or other electronic gadgets, their behaviour may be the same. Parents with children who use technology should restrict their time in front of their screens, participate in activities that don't include their devices, and be present when interacting with their children.

Parenting in the digital age also presents a chance for parents to connect with the children they are raising. Parents may discover common ground with their children and have meaningful interactions with them if they educate themselves on how their children utilize technology and the interests they have in it. This may assist in creating trust between parents and children and deepen the bond between the two.

Being a responsible adult in the digital world is essential to contemporary parenting. It may assist youngsters in maintaining a healthy online presence, developing good habits, and developing critical life skills. Parents with children who use technology need to take the initiative to educate themselves and their children on how to use technology responsibly. Parents who use technology effectively may help their children have a happy and secure experience when they enter the online world by setting an excellent example in terms of how they interact with technology and by having meaningful dialogues with them.

TWO

Challenges to Digital Parenting

The act of guiding one's children through the many applications of technology and the internet is called "digital parenting." It assists children in navigating the digital world while protecting their safety and encouraging the development of their healthy selves. Parenting in the digital age has become more difficult due to the ongoing development of technology. This essay will discuss some difficulties associated with being a parent in the digital age.

Adjusting Your Schedule Accordingly

Maintaining a healthy screen time balance is one of the most challenging difficulties of parenting in the digital age. Youngsters spend much time in front of screens, whether watching television, playing video games, or using mobile devices. This trend is expected to continue. A child's physical and mental health may suffer if they spend excessive time in front of a screen, even though technology has numerous positive consequences. Parents with children who use technology need to monitor their children's screen time and encourage them to participate in activities that don't involve screens, such as sports, socializing, and other pursuits.

Administration of material accessed online.

Managing information online is another obstacle for parents who raise their children in a digital world. The material found on the internet is vast, and some may not be suitable for children or even be detrimental to them. Parents are responsible for supervising their children's internet use and preventing them from seeing anything deemed improper. Parents are also responsible for teaching their children how to use the internet responsibly and securely.

Keeping children safe from dangers they may encounter online

Children are at considerable risk from sexual predators who operate online. They attract youngsters into participating in improper conduct via gaming platforms, social networking platforms, and other online technologies. Parents who use technology should teach their children how to recognize and avoid dangerous people online. Parents are also obligated to monitor what their children are doing online and ensure that their children's social media accounts have stringent privacy settings.

Cyberbullying

One such obstacle that digital parenting might provide is cyberbullying. It includes intimidating or harassing someone via the use of technology. Children who are the targets of cyberbullying may be at risk for various mental health problems, including anxiety, depression, and others. Parents who are active online have a responsibility to teach their children how to identify and report instances of cyberbullying. In addition to this, they should monitor their children's actions online and to urge them to discuss any cases of bullying that they may have seen.

Teaching responsible use of modern technologies

The concept of "digital citizenship" relates to the use of technology and the internet in a responsible manner. It entails showing consideration for the people you interact with online, guarding the privacy of your own information, and making good and productive use of technology. Parents who use technology should demonstrate responsible conduct for their children and educate them the significance of becoming good digital citizens. In addition to this, they are responsible for educating their children about the repercussions of engaging in harmful online conduct such as cyberbullying or posting stuff that is unsuitable.

Keeping abreast on the most recent technological developments

Since technological advances occur at such a rapid rate, it is essential for digital parents to be current on all of the most recent trends and tools. Parents have a responsibility to be knowledgeable about the mobile applications, video games, and social networking sites that their children use. This demands parents to maintain their knowledge and engage in continuing research, in addition to maintaining open lines of communication with their children.

Seeking a happy medium between personal protection and freedom of expression

Parents who have children who use digital devices have the responsibility of balancing the need to safeguard their children's safety with their children's right to privacy. Parents have a responsibility to keep an eye on what their children are doing online and to ensure that their children's social media accounts have adequate privacy settings. Yet, they must also respect the need for privacy that their children have and trust that their children will make appropriate judgments while they are online.

Finding Your Way Across the Digital Divide

The disparity that exists between people who have access to modern technology and those who do not is referred to as the "digital divide." Youngsters who do not have access to modern technologies run the risk of falling farther behind in their academics and missing out on valuable chances. Parents who are digitally literate have a responsibility to help close the digital gender gap by ensuring that their children have access to technology and the internet.

Establishing and maintaining positive interactions with various forms of technology.

Parenting in the digital age requires fostering positive ties with many forms of technology. This entails instructing children on how to utilize technology in a manner that is beneficial to their well-being and encourages them to behave in a constructive manner. Parents who have a digital presence should demonstrate positive behavior for their children by limiting the amount of time they spend in front of screens and placing a higher value on in-person communication.

Establishing credibility

Building trust with one's children is an important last step in digital parenting. Parents who have children who use technology have a responsibility to speak honestly with their children, set rules and limits, and be prepared to listen to their children's concerns. Digital parents may create a supportive and secure environment for their children by establishing trust.

THREE

Parenting Secrets

Secret # 1
Believe in PARENTING Power! Enjoy the blessing you have received as a PARENT.
Be proud and stay Fit! A GOOD PARENTING CAUSES HEADACHES BUT BAD PARENTING CAUSES HEARTACHES

Secret # 2
Get ready for the most demanding job: Parenting is the most demanding job that you have ever done or will be doing. Get ready to learn the tricks of the trade. Be prepared for different situations.

Secret # 3
Lean "how to do caring for the baby" Parenting begins from pregnancy. Once you are pregnant, you will have to stop smoking and drinking. You have to avoid tea and coffee. You need to eat healthy food, get enough rest and so on.

Secret # 4
Learn from experienced parents: If you are a first-time parent, there is much to learn from people who have already raised kids. Your parents can teach you so many things.

Secret # 5
Learn to Stop complaining: Your child may not follow you, but this does not mean you should start complaining. When you make complaints, your child's ego will be hurt.
Good parent loves their child for who they are, not who they will be.

Secret # 6
Keep your expectations high: You should always have high expectations about your child; this will boost confidence in your child. Good parent allows their children to be responsible for their behaviour.

Secret # 7
Encourage your child to take reasonable risks: Risk-taking is suitable for personal development, so you should encourage your child to take reasonable risks. We must treat our

kids as our equals and not as subordinates.

Secret # 8
Don't react immediately: When your child makes mistakes, don't react immediately. Analyze the situation thoroughly before you react. Love your child no matter what. No one is perfect; we have all made mistakes and will continue to.

Secret # 9
Give your children appropriate ways to feel powerful. Let your kid do his own struggle: Struggle is a vital mantra to succeed in life, don't make things easier for the child.

Secret # 10
Keep everything real: Don't lie to your child, let him understand how things are in the real world. If your child is testing you through.... A temper tantrum, anger, crying, disrespect.... It is best to leave the room and tell him to talk to him later.

Secret # 11
Listen to your kids: When your kid wants to say something, don't ignore him. Stop what you

are doing and actively listen to him. Don't interrupt, express your opinion only after he stops. Be firm YET kind!

Secret # 12

Talk to your child: Don't wait for your child to strike the communication. Ask him questions, and encourage him to ask a question. MOM & DAD: "Do not compare me to other children consistently, it makes me jealous."

Secret # 13

Be communicative: Always find time for communication, and never disconnect your kid's call. Communication helps you understand your child as well as helps him to understand his parent.

Secret # 14

Show Good Judgment: Teach what is right and what is wrong. Make them follow the right things and avoid doing wrong. Never try to motivate your child by withdrawing your love.

Secret # 15

Stick to Your Rules: When you make a rule, you should stick to these rules. If you don't follow the rules, how can you expect your child to follow the rules? Never give in to pleas, tears, demands or pouting.

Secret # 16

Become a role model: If you want your kid to be good, you should be a good person yourself. The kids are always watching you, never doing anything wrong in front of them.

Secret # 17

Control your emotions: If you express extreme emotions (anger, frustrations etc.) in front of your child, your child will likely copy that (believe me, children are good at imitating).

Secret # 18

Let them imitate: Human beings learn by imitation, in fact, imitation is the first learning method. Encourage skill development through imitation.

Secret # 19

Show Love: Children are not very good at deciphering the meaning behind words. Therefore, a simple "I love you" does not mean anything to them. Show them your love through hugs, kisses, and even gifts.

Secret # 20
Be positive: If you are positive, your child will grow into an optimistic individual. You might fail at something, however, don't should your failures. Mom & Dad: " Simply correct the mistakes I make instead of yelling at me."

Secret # 21
Avoid negativity: If you are a negative person, your child might grow into a pessimistic individual. If you show your positive side, your child will not incorporate negativity.

Secret # 22
Make them feel secure: Your child should understand you as a safe haven. They need to feel confident around you. Let your child feel that he is safe with you.

Secret # 23
Build trust: If you want your child to rely on

you, you should build trust. If he shares his secret, don't reveal it to anyone, not even your partner.

Secret # 24
Reflect on your experience: Your childhood experience can help you in your parenting journey. If there were things that you liked, implement those things. If you had a bad experience, avoid those things.

Secret # 25
Share your life experience: The child can learn so many things from you as parents. Tell your kids everything you know, how you did certain things, how you behaved and how you nourished with time.

Secret # 26
Find time for yourself: Don't be too harsh on yourself, becoming a good parent does not mean you don't care about your well-being. If you are happy with yourself, you can make your child happy.

Secret # 27
Don't spank: If you spank, your child will learn to become violent. Mom & Dad: "Encourage me to finish my homework. Don't threaten me. It makes me dislike studies."

Secret # 28
Read your child: In order to understand your child, you need to understand child psychology. Try to analyze how your child feels and thinks. Respect his opinion too!

Secret # 29
Read books: There is a lot of research on parenting, read books on parenting and try to implement what you have learned. Mom & Dad: "When you show faith in me, it develops a whole lot of courage in me".

Secret # 30
Talk to other parents: Experienced parents will always have something important to tell you. Mom & Dad: "Give me little chores to do and help out at home. It teaches me life skills."

Secret # 31
Let them be: Don't ask your child to be someone, always encourage them to be themselves. Don't tell them to be like his friend Ravi," instead, help them to be Shashank (your child's name).

Secret # 32
Understand your privilege: The child is a gift of God, understand your privilege as a parent. The child did not arrive to torture you, but instead to make you happy.

Secret # 33
Don't make them act like adults: A child grows into an adult. It is a natural process. Let your child remain a child, don't expect them to act like adults. You don't expect an adult to behave like a child, why should you expect your child to act like an adult?

Secret # 34
Teach survival skills: Life is full of surprises; you never know what comes next. Therefore, make your child ready for various circumstances, for instance, teach them what to do when earthquakes come, or when a stranger approaches and alike.

Secret # 35
Let them learn: You are certainly more knowledgeable than your child, but your child is not ignorant, he has his intelligence. Let him know things in his way. The more they learn the more they earn in life.

Secret # 36
Nurture your child's natural spirituality: Let your child grow naturally into his spiritual understanding, and let him learn from his surroundings. Practice Experiential Learning with the kids.

Secret # 37
Don't meddle: Do you like people meddling in your own business? Certainly not. A child has his world, don't Create an atmosphere of

meddling.

Secret # 38

Create a supporting atmosphere: Do you want your child to live in fear? Create an atmosphere where the child can do what he wants. Letting him do whatever he wants does not mean, the child is allowed to commit wrongs all the time.

Secret # 39

Let the child be free: The thinking that you are his parent and you will never harm him has given birth to the thought that you should control your kids. Too much control is terrible.

Secret # 40
Give them true love: True love is not connected with showering your child with kisses or giving everything your child wants. True love means, you are doing what is best for him.

Secret # 41
Create a loving atmosphere: If you are harsh on your child, he will never trust you, he might even hate you. Never ever compare your one child with the other. Each child is a creative genius.

Secret # 42
Teach your kids about TAXES! Eat 30% of their ICE Cream.
Mom & Dad: "When I am throwing a huge tantrum, at times, all I need is a big hug."

Secret # 43
Don't boss around: Don't judge the child from an ivory tower, instead sit below the child and try to understand his mind.

Secret # 44
Make yourself attractive: If you can attract your

child, he will like you. When he wants you, he will follow you.

Secret # 45
Give love, take affection: Love is a two-way process, if you want to be loved, you must give love. Love your child, and he will shower with affection.

Secret # 46
Respect your child to be respected: Like love, respect is also a two-way process. If you respect your child, the child will certainly respect you.

Secret# 47
Spend quality time: In order to understand your child, you should spend quality time. If you spend quality time, you will also develop a friendship bond with your child.

Secret# 48
Manage your stress: Parenting can be very stressful. When you are too stressed out, you might be a little harsh on the child. Manage your stress, so that you don't spew your

frustration on the child.

Secret # 49
Manage your anger: Most of us cannot avoid anger, however, when you are with your child, you need to control your anger. If you cannot stop yourself from slamming the door, your child will learn how to slam the door and when to slam the door.

Secret # 50
Develop a healthy relationship with your partner: A good parent is an individual who has a good relationship with his/her partner. If you have a healthy relationship with your spouse, your child will grow up in a healthy environment.

Secret # 51
Give them autonomy: The child is small yet has a distinct personality and individuality.

Secret # 52
Let them be independent: You are his parent, and you want your child to be the best, however, does the child want to do what you want him to do? Encourage the child to become self-reliant.

Secret # 53
Provide them opportunities: Let your child explore his hobbies, interests, and skills by giving them options.

Secret # 54
Provide a learning environment: Don't expect your child to pick up his textbook when you switch the TV on.

Secret # 55
Generate good income: You need money for education, upbringing, and medical bills.

Secret # 56
Save money: If you care about your child, you should start saving money and make plans for a better future.

Secret # 57
Behavioural management: Make punishment the last option. Discipline should be used only when all methods of behavioural control have failed.

Secret # 58
Punish your child, but don't be too harsh: Research on parenting and child psychology tells us that sometimes punishment is necessary to discipline the child, enforce rules, and encourage learning.

Secret # 59
Give them nutritious food: The child can be very selective about what they eat, encouraging them to eat healthy food.

Secret # 60

Maintain a healthy lifestyle: Go to bed early, and wake up early. Don't hang out late at night, and don't spend too much time at parties. How you live matters to your child.

Secret # 61
Exercise regularly: Teach your child the importance of exercise and take him jogging or cycle.

Secret # 62
Teach tolerance: we live in a multicultural society, and people from various cultures live among us. Teach your child how to appreciate people from other cultures.

Secret # 63
Teach religion: It is ok to encourage your child to participate in spiritual or religious activities; however, don't force religious guidance. Teach your kids to RESPECT All RELIGIONS.

Secret # 64
Keep an eye on: You should be aware of your child's activities in school, in after-school programs, and community activities.

Secret # 65
Know your child's friends: You should know your child's friends and the parents of your child's friends. Your child's friend can tell you so many things about your child.

Secret # 66
Take precautions to protect your child: Danger is lurking around. Even a simple swing can be dangerous. Watch your child's back.

Secret# 67
Take the helm: Don't let the child dictate you. Once you play by his rules out of love, there will be no turning back. Therefore, let the child know you are in charge.

Secret # 68
Set a boundary: The world can be very

confusing for your child, therefore, set a boundary so your child can explore his passion in a safe environment.

Secret # 69
Don't hurt his self-esteem: Your child is a distinct individual; he has his self-esteem. You don't want anyone to hurt your self-respect, do you?

Secret # 70
Don't clip your child's wings: If your child wants to do things like tying the shoelace, wearing the shirt etc., let him do it. This is good for you as well.

Secret# 71
Never try to fix everything. Let your child find his solution. Don't meddle until he gives up. By giving the child to find his answers, you are teaching him self-reliance and resilience.

Secret # 72
Discipline your child: Disciplining the child begins at home. You should make standard rules on what is and is not allowed.

Secret # 73
Remember, discipline is not about exercising restriction: Your child needs discipline. However, discipline does not mean restricting them. Disciplining means letting them behave appropriately to become a good person.

Secret # 74
Discourage violence: Children are naturally destructive; they enjoy throwing things, and breaking things. You should discourage violence early on.

Secret # 75
Don't make too many rules: Children cannot absorb too many rules. Focus on the things that matter, such as study time, playtime and dinner time, with Tech-Candy Time on their priority!

Secret # 76
Don't be rude: If you are rude to your children, it is very likely that they will also become rude to you. If you talk rudely, they will also speak rudely. If you behave rudely, children will also behave rudely.

Secret # 77
Be polite: Children will understand you when you are polite. If you are impolite, they may follow you in the beginning; however, later, they will become a rebel.

Secret # 78
Understand the age group: Your child passes through various stages; you should understand these ages and treat them accordingly. Parenting a baby is different from parenting a toddler.

Secret # 79
Treat them like a person: Children are also distinct personalities. They want respect, they want to be understood, and they want to be heard.

Secret # 80
Give them choices: You should not force your children to do want you want them to do. Give them options; for instance, let them choose whether to read a storybook, play a video game or even enjoy their cloud presence!

Secret # 81
Spend quality time: Children want your time, they want you to be around them, and they want you to participate in their activities. Therefore, you must have time for your children.

Secret # 82
Give them books: Books are the source of knowledge. Encourage children to read books. When they are reading, pick up your book and sit with them reading your book.

Secret # 83
Read aloud to children: You can encourage reading habits by reading aloud to your children. You read a paragraph and ask your child to read. Children love to listen to their parents. Reading together creates a bonding.

Secret # 84
Interact with the child: Interaction is the key to emotional development. You need to ask many questions and get ready to answer your child's questions.

Secret # 85
Give them interactive toys: Interactive toys can entertain children and help them learn so many things. Things like building blocks will help them learn alphabet and numerals.

Secret # 86
Schedule a play time: Children do not like seriousness; therefore, instead of reading books, they are likely to watch cartoon. Schedule a play time. You might tell them they can play the game once they finish breakfast.

Secret # 87
Let them see things: Seeing is believing. Instead of telling them what a tiger is or showing a video of a tiger, take them to the zoo and let them see a real tiger. Practice experiential learning on routine.

Secret # 88
Go for co-parenting: Mother and father are both responsible for taking care of the child. This is imperative for the emotional well-being of the child. Not just mothers, fathers also should take an interest in parenting.

Secret # 89
Daddy time: Generally speaking, dads are usually not involved in parenting. Dads don't feed their children; they don't clean their children. Research tells kids that are taken care of by dads to excel in school and develop problem-solving skills.

Secret # 90
Mummy time: In most cases, moms are the ones who are around the children all the time. This might bore the children. Moms should create special activities to engage children.

Secret # 91
Create warm memories: You sure have warm memories from childhood, don't you? Do you remember when your day read stories to you? Do you remember when you and your mom played a board game?

Secret # 92
Create exciting activities: Boredom grabs children quickly. The toy they loved a week ago will no longer interest them. Create interesting activities. Simple things like bathing a dog can be fascinating to children or even watering plants!

Secret # 93
Become a great cook: Children are very choosy about what they eat. One of the common problems for mothers is feeding their child. Learn cooking and always try new dishes.

Secret # 94
Let them enter the kitchen: Cooking is a fun activity for children. Your child will enjoy cooking with you. Don't let them play with a knife or go near the stove. However, you can ask them to beat the egg, sort out vegetables and arrange the table. Why not?

Secret# 95
Go for gardening: Children love to play with mud and water. Take them to the garden and help them sow the seeds, water the plants and explore nature!

Secret # 96
Bring a pet into your home: Children love animals and birds. Having a dog, a cat, a parrot, and even a fish in the house will make your children happy. Children love interacting with living things more than non-living things like a toy car.

Secret # 97
Admit your mistakes: When you admit your mistakes, your children will learn to apologize when they commit wrongs. Admitting your

mistakes in front of your child will not diminish your personality.

Secret # 98
Go for a nature walk: Nature can teach your child many things. You can tell your child how trees help human beings, how human beings are dependent on the ecosystem and even share the geography around!

Secret # 99
Teach them to care for the environment: Tell your child how the background relates to human beings. Teach them not to waste, and tell them to reuse things. For example, you can say to him how water is essential and why he should not use waste water.

Secret # 100
Encourage social responsibility: Picking trash from the garden might sound boring. However, your child might love this if you make this a game.

Secret # 101
Teach them compassion: Help your child understand the power of compassion. Encourage

them to be compassionate towards homeless people, animals and the poor.

Secret # 102
Always tell the truth: What kind of child will you bring up if you don't speak the truth? If you want your child to behave right, you should always talk about the truth. By telling the truth, you will be bringing a morally responsible individual.

Secret # 103
Don't lie to your child: If you continuously lie to your children, your child will stop believing you. If you lie, your child will no more respect you, no more love you. Even white lies can be very damaging.

Secret # 104
Attend all the PTMs, School Functions, and Get Together moments at school without fail. When both MOM and DAD go to school together, the kids love it!

Secret # 105

Don't nag with your partner: Children raised in families where partners quarrel are likely to develop into a weak personalities. It is widespread to disagree with your partner. If you ever happen to argue, always do it when the children are not around.

Secret # 106
Praise in public and criticize in Private. The same goes for your spouse and the kids! Remember this without fail!

Secret # 107
Respect your partner: In families where the women have a high opinion of their men and vice versa, the children will also have a high idea of their dads and moms. When you respect your partner, your child will love his dad and mom more.

Secret # 108
Respect the parenting differences: Your idea of parenting might differ from your partner's. You need to support your spouse's parenting method because he/she does not mean any harm to the child.

Secret # 109
Praise your child: When your child does something good, praise him. When you praise them, they will be encouraged to do better. Even when he is not doing well, you must praise him for attempting it.

Secret # 110
Always give positive feedback: A child needs positive feedback. Telling her that the drawing is crap will make her feel worse. Instead of saying the picture is terrible, you must say, "If you erase this line and draw another curve here, the drawing will be better."

Secret # 111
Avoid negative feedback: Children are easily discouraged by negative feedback. When you give negative feedback a child might lose interest in attempting the same thing again. Even if your child comes home with an "E" grade, don't give negative feedback to his face.

Secret # 112
Reward your child: Rewards have a tremendous effect on human psychology, even more on children. Reward your child for his

achievement. You can tell him he will have a bicycle if he gets an "A" in the following exams.

Secret # 113
Cherish his achievements: Your child comes home with good grades, and show your appreciation. If your child wins a trophy in a race, place the award alongside your valuables.

Secret # 114
Watch him perform: If your child participates in any competition, attend the event. If he makes it, hug him, kiss him. If he does not make it, praise him for participating.

Secret # 115
Make him feel special: Your child is very special to you; however, does your child know this? You have to make your child feel special each time and every time!

Secret # 116
Gossip about your child: It makes more sense when your child finds you saying good things about him to dad than in front of him.

Secret # 117
Trust Yourself: You know your child better than anyone; always trust your gut. Even if you think you are wrong, you are likely right.

Secret # 118
Know when to say YES and when to say NO: Disciplining a child can be adamant; you should know when to say yes and no.

Secret # 119
Say NO when your child is distrustful and intolerant: Don't let your child become disrespectful to you or anyone else. Stop him when he becomes intolerant.

Secret # 120
Build confidence: You can build confidence in your child by praising and rewarding his

achievements. You can also build confidence in the child by participating in his activities.

Secret # 121
Let him channel emotions: If your child is angry, divert his mind by asking him to participate in exciting activities. If your child is crying, make him feel secure by hugging him tight.

Secret # 122
Teach your kids. EMPATHY by telling them stories of your age/life with moral lessons.

Secret # 123
Empower yourself with the power of TECHNOLOGY to match the requirements of the KIDS at home!

Secret # 124
Teach ethics: Teach your child what is ethical and what is unethical. Help him understand the difference between ethical and unethical.

Secret # 125
Teach morality: Morality is a distinction between good and evil; morality refers to the proper conduct. By teaching morality, try to raise a morally responsible individual.

Secret # 126
Tell them the importance of values: Explain to your child why being good matters, and how truthfulness will help in life.

Secret # 127
Don t fight when your child does not eat: Food fight is widespread. If your child does not eat a particular food, offer him another dish or ask him what he wants to eat. If he does not want to eat, let it be. Your child will not starve.

Secret # 128
Make a parenting schedule: parenting is hard work; it can exhaust you thoroughly. Making a schedule can ease your work. Set a timetable for various responsibilities.

Secret # 129
Encourage your kids to do creative things: Ask your child to sing, dance, write, draw, and play instruments. Creative activities like these will boost his mental capacity.

Secret # 130
Encourage physical activities: Research shows that brain development is connected with physical activity. Encourage your children to walk, run, and play outdoor games.

Secret # 131
Take your child to regular medical checkups: You should get all the required vaccines for your child. You also need to take your child to the doctor regularly. Never ignore health-related complaints.

Secret # 132
Take care of personal hygiene: Encourage your child to brush their teeth, wash his hands and feet, take a bath regularly. Learning should be made a habit rather than an occasional occurrence.

Secret # 133
Be vigilant about safety: Always ensure the babies and toddlers are not left alone. Tell him to wear a helmet when riding his bike or scooter.

Secret # 134
Think twice before administering drugs: Antibiotics can cause problems; therefore, always look for alternatives.

Secret # 135
Promote independence: Your child's development will be hindered if he is too dependent on you. You need to tell him that you are always with him, yet make him go alone.

Secret # 136
Never push too far: Have high expectations. Expect your child to do great things, tell him to aim high, but, never go him too far.

Secret # 137
Let your child try: Resist doing what your child can do herself. Your child might take 30 minutes

to eat his meal by himself and if you spoon-feed, you may do it in 10 minutes, however, by not letting your child do it on his own, you are hindering his learning process.

Secret # 138
Don't redo what your child has already done: Unless it is very necessary, don't fix what your child has already done. This will discourage your child to do it on her own.

Secret # 139
Let them solve the problems: What do you do when you see your child trying to get a toy from the shelf that she is finding hard to reach? If you want to get it for her, just stop.

Secret # 140
Give your child an assignment: Encourage your child to do things like sorting out the coloured dresses for the laundry, picking books from the floor, and picking the trash from the garden.

Secret # 141
Develop a routine: Make a routine for your child to read books, do his assignments, play games and watch TV. Give him or her a say in your

daily routine.

Secret # 142
Develop predictable routines: When the children follow the same way every day, they learn quickly. The routine should include things like brushing teeth before going to bed, washing hands before eating and offering prayers at least once a day.

Secret # 143
Encourage cooperation: Make your child understand that human beings are social animals and that cooperation is the key to becoming successful. Teach teamwork by asking your child to get along with his peers.

Secret # 144
Teach manners: Children are deft in throwing tantrums. One of the ways to control tempers is by teaching them manners. You have to teach them how to behave well.

Secret # 145
Make rules: You need to make rules and make

your child strictly follow these rules. The rules for the children can be as simple as "do not litter around" or as complex as "do not talk to strangers."

Secret # 146
Be funny and humorous: Sometimes you are required to make faces to make your child laugh, and sometimes you are required to dress funnily to make your child smile.

Secret # 147
Teach time management: You should teach your child when to stop watching TV, when to stop playing a video game and when to go to bed.

Secret # 148
Use infographics and images to teach your child: Research tells us that children learn faster if infographics and images are used. Give them picture books to help them understand things.

Secret # 149
Let them watch instructional and educational videos: Children learn faster when they watch

instructional and educational videos.

Secret # 150
Use child-friendly language: Tell your child "If you finish your homework, we might go to the park." Or, "Finish your homework, and we'll go to the park." You can see the difference in reactions.

Secret # 151
Don't use vulgar words: Never use curse words, or vulgar words in front of the child. No "shit" no "IDIOT". Make them aware of the signs of CHILD ABUSE too!

Secret # 152
Don't compare your child with another child: When you begin to compare your child with another child, jealousy and enmity will develop.

Secret # 153
Have a movie time: Everyone needs entertainment? Take your child to the movie, or have a movie time at home.

Secret # 154
Play music: Music will not only unburden your exhausted mind but also make your child happy.

Secret # 155
Encourage teamwork: What if children are fighting over the same toy? You can tell one child to play for 10 minutes and then give it to another to play for 10 minutes.

Secret # 156
Let your child settle his own dispute: If the children are debating, don't interfere unless one of them goes violent. Let the children settle their own disputes.

Secret # 157
Learn how to divert your child's mind. If your child is drawing on the wall, bring chart paper and ask him to draw on the paper.

Secret # 158
Learn to manage good-bye meltdowns: Your child may not want to leave you and go to

school. Give him something like your picture, a heart-shaped tissue to make him feel that you are with him.

Secret # 159
Help them in righting their wrongs: When your child tears papers and throw them over the floor, ask him to collect the pieces and throw them in the dustbin. Make " Sorry" and "Thank you" their favourite language.

Secret # 160
Reprimand immediately: If your child does something wrong, reprimand them immediately. Don't wait until you get home.

Secret # 161
Make sure they get enough sleep: Children are very proactive, they need rest. Research says if a sixth-grader child loses one hour of sleep, his intelligence will be reduced to that of a fourth-grader.

Secret # 162
Raise honest kids: Honesty is the best policy is an old saying. However, research has proved that when a child is real, he will grow up into

a responsible human being. Your child might lie in order to please you or get benefits. Always check whether the child is telling truth or not.

Secret # 163

You need rules: Kids need directions, and so do you. Setting rules for kids also means you have your own rules to follow. If you don't want your kid to watch TV late at night, you also need to avoid watching TV late at night.

Secret # 164

Too much control is terrible: The kids whose parents are too strict are the ones who do drugs, drink and smoke. Never do so in front of them ever too!

Secret # 165

Don't let boredom get into your child: If you are too busy for your child, your child might be bored. When a child is bored, he will try to take refuge in activities such as smoking, drinking, and drugs.

Secret # 166

Get into healthy arguments: Research has shown that moderate argument has a positive effect on children.

Secret # 167

Teach them to be grateful: Being grateful is excellent quality. Your children must learn how to express gratitude.

Secret # 168

Create the right atmosphere: You need to have a child-friendly environment in your house. Creating the right atmosphere is a big part of parenthood. The right atmosphere implies happiness, love, compassion, and discipline.

Secret # 169

Don't impose your dream: You might have wanted to become a doctor but ended by being a salesperson. Don't put pressure on your child to fulfil your dream.

Secret # 170

Know what the child needs: You have a business and you see your child as your successor. This is quite reasonable. However, does your child want to follow in your footsteps?

Secret # 171

Don't pamper: It is true that you need to make your child feel special. However, if you are too much bragging about your child, you are spoiling him.

Secret # 172

Be ready to learn from your child: As a parent, you are the first teacher for your child. However, there are so many things that your child can teach you. Having a child means you are ready to learn so many things.

Secret # 173

Be joyful: Nobody forced you to become a parent, it was your own choice. If you are showing tension, anger, fear, anxiety, and jealousy every now and then, what will the child learn?

Secret # 174

Improving behavioural problems in children: Toddlers show tantrums, and teens are rebellious by nature. You cannot solve behavioural issues in children until you understand their minds and know what exactly they want. Communicate as much as you can to sort out the issues.

Secret # 175

Learn how to entertain the children: If you can keep the children busy, you will win the battle to keep them quiet. There are various ways to engage your child, find out what's your child's favourite.

Secret # 176

Go for outings: Like you, children also get bored with routine life, then they to tours to make life enjoyable. This will also create a deep bonding.

Secret # 177

Organize children's parties: In order to show how much you love him, you need to organize children's parties and invite your child's friends. Parties are suitable for the children as well as parents as they encourage social interactions amongst the parents.

Secret # 178

Check the development process: Make sure you are aware of the changes in your children's bodies. Guide them about the changes in their personality, and character and impart them about SEX EDUCATION before they learn from the outside world.

Secret # 179
Check the learning process: Find out how your child is learning. Look into his notebooks, school reports and homework. Never guide them to their homework directly. Have an eye on their study routine.

Secret # 180
Find out if someone is bullying your child: Bullying can be detrimental to mental development. Find out whether your child is being bullied in the neighbourhood or at school.

Secret # 181
Find out whether your child is struggling with cyberbullying: It is very common to see children as young as 5 years use the internet. Check for the signs of cyberbullying.

Secret # 182

Check your children's online activities: The Internet is a source of information and knowledge. However, there are also many bad things about the internet. Be aware of their user IDs' and Passwords. A Good Parent is a Friend of their kids on Social Networking Sites.

Secret # 183
Exercise parental control on cable TV: TV is a good source of learning and entertainment. However, TV also brings channels that can harm the child.

Secret # 184
Exercise parental control on the internet: In order to stop children from checking porn sites and other illegal sites, you need to block malicious sites.

Secret # 185
Do not let them choose friends over parents: When it comes to confiding in something, children will always go to their friends. However, their friends are not the best people to give them advice. You can be your childhood friends and encourage them to confide in you.

Secret # 186
Let them choose their own career: You know what is best for your children. However, what you think is the best might not be the best for them. Advise them, but let them take their own path.

Secret # 187
Make yourself available: When your children need you, you must always be available. One mistake can damage their entire life. Respect your parents before your KIDS.

Secret # 188
Don't make them feel they can have it all: Don't make things easier for your kid. They need to understand things are also not easier for parents.

Secret # 189
Teach the value of money: Money has great importance in life. Teach your children it is not easy to make money. If you are giving pocket money, check how they are spending.

Secret # 190
Teach them to spend less, and save more: If they learn how hard it is to make money, they will learn the importance of spending less and saving more.

Secret # 191
Happy families don't happen by accident. They are born from intentional parenting. Make sure you as a parent value the family meal and car rides.

Secret # 192
Learn to move on: One day your child becomes a teen and is ready to leave the house (for work, education etc.). Your child is your child, whether he is one month old or 50 years old.

Secret # 193
Don't compromise your own well-being: Your children are your blood and bones, however, you should never compromise your well-being. Taking care of children does not mean you have to forget about yourself.

Secret # 194
You don't own your children: One of the main issues of conflict between the parents and children is because of the sense of ownership in parents. Parents tend to think their children like their pets. Give them freedom of LIVING.

Secret # 195
Get support from others: There is no five-point guide to parenting. Everyone has his/her own parenting style. If you are having difficulty, you can join a parents group and ask for help.

Secret # 196
Raise a giver: There is so much pleasure in giving. Teach your child to become a giver. Let your child understand the importance of giving. Remember YOU just can not raise as you were raised!

Secret # 197
Don't let them get away with meanness: Children can be very mean. They are likely to do emotional blackmailing. Be involved in their lives.

Secret # 198

Ask your kids to help you: When you need extra hands for household work, ask your children to volunteer. This will make your children respond to the family needs. Frequently ask them to do Car Wash or water the plants together.

Secret # 199

Don't yell: Generally speaking, yelling will produce a parent-deaf kid. This shall also cause a dislike with either of the parents by the kid for life.

Secret # 200

Move close, but give them privacy: You need to be close to your kids, but you also should give them privacy. Know their friends and observe their routine. Never bridge their interest but feed their likes.

FOUR

Poem on Digital Parenting

In this world of screens and devices, Parenting has new surprises. It's no longer just about the

birds and bees, But also about online safety and cyber needs.

Digital parenting is the new norm, A world of rules, restrictions, and forms. We must be vigilant and always on the alarm to protect our children from online harm.

We must teach them to use tech carefully, navigate and beware of cyberbullies, hackers, and fake news, and protect their privacy and views.

We must set limits and boundaries, And make sure our rules are not arbitrary. Screens can be addictive and time-consuming And can hinder growth and learning.

We must encourage face-to-face interactions, And limit screen time and distractions. Children need to play and explore, learn, grow and adore.

Digital parenting is not easy, but we can bask with love, patience, and guidance. I the joy of watching our children thrive, In this digital age, where screens and devices are rife.

FIVE

Song on Digital Parenting

(Verse 1) We're raising kids in the digital sky in a world of screens and Wi-Fi. From smartphones to tablets and laptops, too, It's hard to know just what to do.

(Chorus) Digital parenting is the game's name, Teaching our kids how to use tech without shame. Protecting their hearts and minds from the screen, Guiding them safely is what it means.

(Verse 2) There are social media and online games, Where predators lurk and cyberbully aim. We must teach our kids to be intelligent and strong, To use tech for good, and avoid what's wrong.

(Chorus) Digital parenting is the game's name, Teaching our kids how to use tech without shame. Protecting their hearts and minds from the screen, Guiding them safely is what it means.

(Bridge) We can't shield them from the digital world, But we can help them navigate the swirl. From setting limits to open communication, We can build trust and a strong foundation.

(Chorus) Digital parenting is the game's name, Teaching our kids how to use tech without shame. Protecting their hearts and minds from the screen, Guiding them safely is what it means.

(Outro) We're in this together, as parents and guides, To help our kids thrive, and to stay on the right side. Digital parenting, it's a challenge we face, But with love and care, we'll create a safe space.

SIX

QUOTES ON DIGITAL PARENTING

"It's important to teach our kids about digital citizenship, just as we teach them about good manners and respect." - Leslie Mann, actress and mom.

ᑭᑭᑭ

"As parents, we need to set boundaries for our kids when it comes to digital devices, and also model responsible behaviour ourselves." - Anne-Marie Slaughter, New America President and CEO.

ᑭᑭᑭ

"Digital devices can be wonderful tools for learning, but they need to be used in moderation and with supervision." - Dr Elizabeth Englander, founder and director of the Massachusetts Aggression Reduction Center.

ᑭᑭᑭ

"Parents need to educate themselves on the digital landscape to guide their children through it effectively." - Chris McKenna, founder of the Internet Safety Group.

ÞÞÞ

"Our kids need to know that what they post online can have real-world consequences and that they are responsible for their digital footprint." - Amy Guggenheim Shenkan, CEO of Common Sense Media.

ÞÞÞ

"Digital parenting is not about being a spy or a helicopter parent, but about creating a culture of trust and open communication around technology." - Devorah Heitner, author of Screenwise: Helping Kids Thrive (and Survive) in Their Digital World.

ÞÞÞ

"Parents need to work with schools to develop a comprehensive approach to digital citizenship education so that our kids are prepared for the digital world they will inherit." - Dr Justin Patchin, the Cyberbullying Research Center co-director.

ᑭᑭᑭ

"We need to help our kids balance their online and offline lives so they can develop healthy habits and relationships in both realms." - Vicki Davis, educator and author.

ᑭᑭᑭ

"Digital devices are a tool, not a babysitter. We need to prioritize face-to-face communication and human connection with our kids." - Katie Hurley, LCSW, author of The Happy Kid Handbook.

ᑭᑭᑭ

"As parents, we need to be aware of the risks and benefits of digital devices, and make informed decisions about how we incorporate them into our family's life." - Dr Jenny Radesky, a developmental-behavioural paediatrician and lead author of the American Academy of

Paediatrics guidelines on media use in children.

ᖰᖰᖰ

SEVEN

Jokes on Digital Parenting

Why did digital parents give their children a modem for their birthday? So they could

always stay connected!

ღღღ

What did the digital parent say when their child asked for a new phone? "Let's talk about it... over FaceTime!"

ღღღ

How does a digital parent punish their child for misbehaving online? They take away their mouse and keyboard privileges!

ღღღ

Why did the digital parent hire a cybersecurity expert for their child's birthday party? To make sure there weren't any uninvited guests on the Wi-Fi!

ღღღ

Why did the digital parent go to their child's school to discuss online safety? To show off their impressive PowerPoint skills!

ღღღ

How does a digital parent deal with their child staying up too late on their computer? They turn off the Wi-Fi and say, "Go to sleep; it's time for your hard drive to rest!"

ᑭᑭᑭ

Why did the digital parent cross the road? To get to the other side of the Wi-Fi signal!

ᑭᑭᑭ

What do you call a digital parent who's always on their phone? A "textpert"!

ᑭᑭᑭ

Why did the digital parent refuse to let their child use the computer? They didn't want them to get "keyboard warriors elbow"!

ᑭᑭᑭ

How does a digital parent know their child is sick? They don't ask for their iPad!

ᑭᑭᑭ

EIGHT

Tips to Fostering Healthy Tech-Child Relationship

- *Set boundaries and limits around technology use.*
- *Create a family media plan to help regulate technology use.*
- *Model healthy technology use behaviours for your children.*
- *Monitor your child's technology use.*
-

Encourage face-to-face communication and socialization.

•

Emphasize the importance of physical activity and exercise.

•

Encourage your child to pursue non-screen-related hobbies and interests.

•

Encourage your child to read books for pleasure.

•

Monitor your child's social media accounts and interactions.

•

Teach your child about online privacy and safety.

•

Teach your child about responsible digital citizenship.

•

Set up parental controls on your child's devices.

•

Teach your child about cyberbullying and how to prevent it.

- *Encourage your child to seek help if they experience cyberbullying.*

- *Teach your child about online predators and how to avoid them.*

- *Help your child develop critical thinking skills.*

- *Encourage your child to be creative and express themselves through technology.*

- *Set limits on screen time.*

- *Encourage your child to take regular breaks from technology.*

- *Use technology as a tool for learning and education.*

•

Encourage your child to collaborate with others online.

- *Encourage your child to create and share their content online.*

- *Teach your child about copyright and plagiarism.*

- *Encourage your child to use technology to explore their interests and passions.*

- *Monitor your child's gaming habits and set limits on gaming time.*

- *Teach your child about healthy sleep habits.*

- *Encourage your child to use technology to stay organized and manage their time.*

- *Help your child set goals for technology use.*

- *Encourage your child to use technology to stay in touch with family and friends.*

- *Teach your child about online etiquette and manners.*

- *Encourage your child to use technology to stay informed about current events.*

- *Teach your child about the potential negative effects of excessive technology use.*

- *Encourage your child to use technology to pursue their educational goals.*

- *Help your child develop a healthy relationship with technology.*

- *Encourage your child to use technology to learn a new language.*

- *Teach your child about the importance of digital footprints.*

- *Encourage your child to use technology to explore different cultures.*

-

Monitor your child's use of video-sharing platforms.

•

Encourage your child to use technology to develop problem-solving skills.

•

Encourage your child to use technology to develop creativity.

•

Teach your child about the potential consequences of sharing personal information online.

•

Teach your child about the importance of online reputation.

•

Encourage your child to use technology to pursue their career goals.

•

Monitor your child's use of chat rooms and online forums.

•

Teach your child about the importance of setting strong passwords.

•

Encourage your child to use technology to stay organized and productive.

- *Teach your child about the potential adverse effects of excessive social media use.*

- *Encourage your child to use technology to learn about different perspectives.*

- *Monitor your child's use of messaging apps.*

- *Teach your child about the importance of digital literacy.*

- *Encourage your child to use technology to stay connected with distant relatives.*

- *Teach your child about the importance of backing up their data.*

- *Monitor your child's use of location-sharing apps.*

Encourage your child to use technology to learn about the environment.

- *Teach your child about the importance of respecting others online.*

- *Encourage your child to use technology to explore career opportunities.*

About The Author

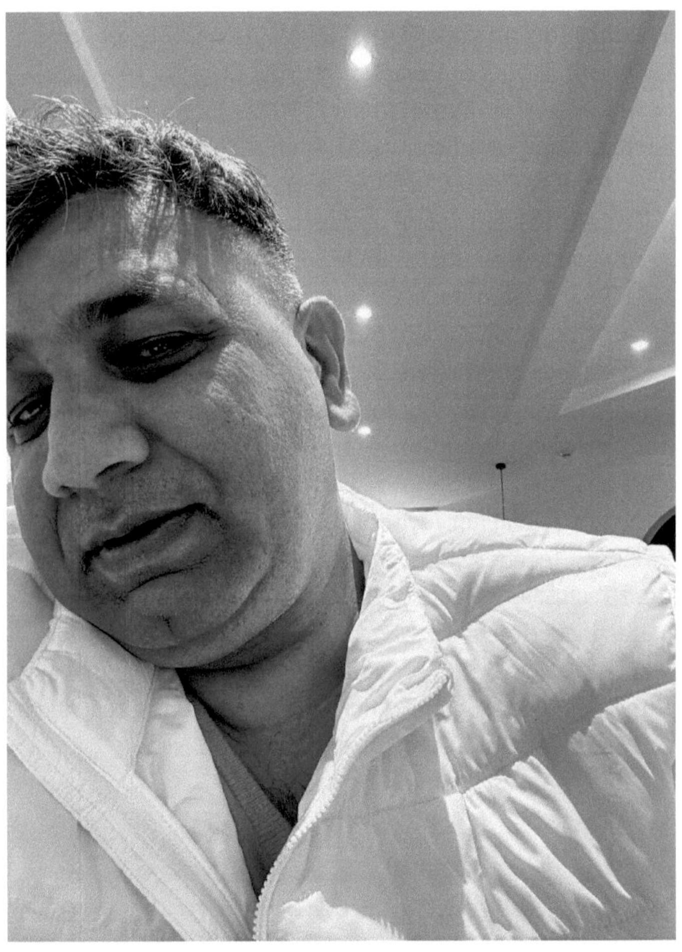

Dheeraj Mehrotra, MS, MPhil, PhD (Education Management) honoris causa., a white and a yellow belt in

SIX SIGMA, a Certified NLP Business Diploma holder, is an Educational Innovator, Author, with expertise in Six Sigma In Education, Academic Audits, Neuro-Linguistic Programming (NLP), Total Quality Management In Education, an Experiential Educator, a CBSE Resource towards School Assessment (SQAA), CCE, JIT, Five S, and KAIZEN. He has authored over 100 books on topics which include Computer Science, AI, Digital Body Language, NLP, Quality Circles, School Management, Classroom Effectiveness and Safety and security in schools. A former Principal at De Indian Public School, New Delhi, (INDIA), NPS International School, Guwahati, and Education Officer at GEMS, Gurgaon, with an ample teaching experience of over Two Decades, he is a certified Trainer for Quality Circles/ TQM in Education and QCI Standards for School Accreditation/ School Audits and Management. He has also been honoured with the President of India's National Teacher Award in the year 2006 and the Best Science Teacher State Award (By the Ministry of Science and Technology, State of UP), Innovation in Education for his inception of Six Sigma In Education by Education Watch, New Delhi. Presently engaged as a Principal at Kunwar's Global School, Lucknow, India. Can be reached at www.authordheerajmehrotra.com

Books By The Same Author

SECURING SAFETY & QUALITY CARING

99 SAFETY AND SECURITY

ANCHORS WITHIN SCHOOLS

DR. DHEERAJ MEHROTRA

A PRIORITY

FOR SCHOOLS

www.authordheerajmehrotra.com

BY NATIONAL
AWARDEE
EDUCATOR
Kindle Price: ₹ 72.00
inclusive of all taxes
Teaching
in the
VUCA
WORLD
Dr. Dheeraj Mehrotra
authordheerajmehrotra.com
Flipkart
available at
amazon

101
SCHOOL
MANAGEMENT
STRATEGIES
Towards EFFECTIVE
QUALITY MANAGEMENT
System in Schools
DR. DHEERAJ
MEHROTRA
Digital List Price: ₹72.45
M.R.P.: ₹199.00
Kindle Price: ₹ 69.00
Save ₹ 130.00 (65%)
inclusive of all taxes
amazon
www.authordheerajmehrotra.com

BOOKS BY THE SAME AUTHOR

Printed by Libri Plureos GmbH in Hamburg,
Germany